MW00826141

Dramatizing Three Classic Tales

 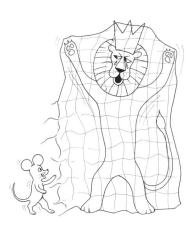 

Smith and Kraus, Inc.
Instructional Books for Teachers Grades K–6

Anyone Can Produce Plays with Kids: The Absolute Basics for Staging Your Own At-Home, In-School, Round-the-Neighborhood Plays by L.E. McCullough

Dramatizing Aesop's Fables: Creative Scripts for the Classroom, Grades K–8 by Louise Thistle

Dramatizing Mother Goose: The Teacher's Guide to Play Acting in the Classroom, Preschool–Grade 2 by Louise Thistle

Dramatizing Myths and Tales: Creating Plays for Large Groups, Grades 3–12 by Louise Thistle

Dramatizing Classic Poetry for Middle and High School Students by Louise Thistle

Movement Stories for Children, Ages 3–6 by Helen Landalf and Pamela Gerke

Moving the Earth: Teaching Earth Science through Movement, Grades 3–6 by Helen Landalf

Moving is Relating: Developing Interpersonal Skills through Movement, Grades 3–6 by Helen Landalf

Hooves and Horns, Fins and Feathers: Drama Curriculum for Grades K–1 by Helen Landalf

Mail and Mystery, Family and Friends: Drama Curriculum for Grades 2–3 by Helen Landalf

If you require prepublication information about upcoming Smith and Kraus books, you may receive our semiannual catalogue, free of charge, by sending your name and address to *Smith and Kraus Catalogue, 4 Lower Mill Road, North Stratford, NH 03590. Or call us at (800) 895-4331, fax (603) 643-1831. WWW.SmithKraus.com.*

Dramatizing Three Classic Tales

The Little Red Hen
The Lion and the Mouse
and
The Three Billy Goats Gruff

Say and Act Stories by Louise Thistle

YOUNG ACTOR SERIES

A Smith and Kraus Book

Dedicated to my aunt, Frances Thistle Nicholson,
my grand nephew, John Lewis Thistle,
and my grand niece, Patricia Ann Thistle.

Published by
Smith and Kraus, Inc.
177 Lyme Road, Hanover, NH 03755
www.SmithKraus.com

Copyright © 2000 by Louise Thistle

All rights reserved. Limited Reproduction Permission:
The publisher grants permission to individual teachers to reproduce the scripts as needed for use with their own
students. Reproduction for an entire school district or for commercial use is prohibited.

First edition: July 2000
10 9 8 7 6 5 4 3 2 1

Book design by Julia Hill Gignoux, Freedom Hill Design
Cover and text illustrations by Emily Packer, Susan Corey, and Louise Thistle

Publisher's Cataloguing-in-Publication Data
Thistle, Louise,
Cramatizing three classic tales : say and act stories / by Louise Thistle.
p. cm. — (Young actors series)
Contents: The little red hen — The lion and the mouse — The three billy goats Gruff.
ISBN 1-57525-192-2
1. Children's plays — Presentations, etc. I. Title. II. Series.
PN3157.T49 2000
792'.0226—dc21   00-032960

CONTENTS

ACKNOWLEDGMENTS

This book would not be possible without the help of many people. First, I thank Emily Packer who has spent hundreds of hours with me on every aspect of this book including major editorial and art suggestions. This book would not be possible without her knowledgeable and creative guidance, encouragement and support.

I thank Rosa Isela Perez and the teachers of Project Excel and Project First Step who welcomed me into their classrooms, gave me important feedback and wonderful opportunities to dramatize with their students.

I appreciate the expert editorial help of Mary Ann Petteway. Dianne Tucker-La Plount gave me valuable suggestions on using this material to appeal to a wide population of students. I am grateful to former Point Loma Librarian Pat Katka, who spent hours obtaining special books for me throughout the library system. For help with research, I thank Jean Stewart, Children's Librarian of the San Diego Public Library and her staff, who efficiently and graciously fulfilled my many requests for books. Librarian Frieda Pallas gave me practical and creative suggestions for making the books appealing to librarians. Thank you to Beverly Cramb for her expert advice on using Bloom's Taxonomy.

I greatly value the art and drama suggestions of director and child drama specialist Sharon Oppenheimer, Ph.D. Jenny Hartman's sensitivity and insights enhance my work. Author-psychologist Jack Sanford provides me with invaluable insight and writing advice.

I offer thanks to Maria and Athan Anagnostopoulos, Directors of The Greek Institute, in Cambridge, Mass. They encouraged me to dramatize Aesop's Fables and showed me the power of the fables to delight and inspire people of all ages and backgrounds. Dan Toporski continually and graciously offers me help with my computer needs. Dudley Hartman comes to the rescue in computer emergencies. Sally Deaton offers continuous encouragement and reinforcement. Meigs Ingham, Manager of the Old Globe Gift Shop in San Diego, makes my work accessible to teachers.

Finally, I thank my husband Charles Francis Dicken, who edits all of my work and gives me creative suggestions and ideas that greatly enrich and enhance it.

TO THE ADULT

These dramatized tales capitalize on children's innate love of language and delight in being physically involved in it. All children, no matter what their language ability, can enjoy and act these stories using their universal language of exuberant vocalization, facial expression and body movement.

Each tale has "Action Pictures" and "Action Phrases" showing what to do. The bold words are phrases for the students to chant.

The tales use a method of dramatization called Narrative Mime Chant. To do Narrative Mime Chant, a narrator tells the story, and the children do actions and chant key words for each sentence in the story. Two ways to do Narrative Mime Chant are:

1. *Everybody acts all the characters:* The teacher does the actions and says the chants along with the children who act with her.

2. *Individuals are cast in roles:* Individuals are cast in roles as in a play. Children also become the inanimate objects such as trees, berry bushes, lakes, river, a bridge, growing wheat, a mill wheel, an oven, etc. A Sound Crew makes sound effects to punctuate the action.

HINTS TO DEVELOP LANGUAGE, DRAMA, AND LITERATURE APPRECIATION

1. Model speaking and acting slowly, and rhythmically. Slow speech helps everyone understand. It is also artistic, teaches good speech and promotes classroom control.

2. Change your voice for each character. Use a strong, low voice for mighty characters; a high, light one for tiny vulnerable ones; a treacherous menacing one for evil enemies; a happy lighthearted one for graceful characters and joyful events.

PROPS AND COSTUMES

Simple props and costumes develop the imagination and are easy to obtain. Costumes and props can be found in thrift stores, garage sales, among your own throwaways, and in variety or party-supply stores.

Use the same pieces again and again, because they need not represent a character or object but may suggest an attribute. For example, sheer blue fabric can be a lake, the sky, or shawl for a princess. A black baseball cap might be a bird, a dog, or a horse with ribbons attached for a mane.

Suggestions for obtaining costume pieces and props:

• Hats make the best costume pieces. Baseball caps and visors can be adapted for animals, insects or birds. Wear the bill forward to create a critter with a snout or bill. Ears may be attached. Turn the bill around for snoutless critters.

• Shawls may become birds' wings, a hunter's net, the swaying branches of a palm tree, and skirts or cloaks for maids young and old.

- Gloves can become puppets. Wear gloves of various colors to become berry bushes, flowers, grains of wheat, or wiggling green grass.

- Fabrics worn or maneuvered create wonderful scenic effects. Lightweight fabrics that move well are easy to store. For example, wiggle blue nylon fabric to create a rippling river or sparkling lake. Tie yellow nylon netting around the head to become the sun or fling it over a lion as a net.

SOUND EFFECTS

Enhance a dramatization with the use of rhythm instruments to create sound effects. For example, strike a drum to simulate a lion pawing; shake jingle bells for swaying trees, a meowing cat, or frolicking goats.

The following instruments create many effects:

        drum
        six-inch triangle
        jingle bells, handbell
        wind chimes
        tambourine
        guiro (large wooden, fish-shaped scraper with a striker)
        rhythm sticks
        shakers (such as maracas or calabash rattles)
        wood block with a mallet.

Instruments particularly suited for students grade two and below are a drum, wood block, rhythm sticks, tambourine, and jingle bells. West Music Company, 1212 5th St. Coralville, IA 52241, (800-397-9378) has a catalog with a wide range of instruments at reasonable prices, or use the yellow pages.

STORY QUESTIONS AND ACTIVITIES

The end of each story has Critical Thinking Questions, Moral Reasoning Questions, and Across the Curriculum Activities. In addition, an Activity Sheet lets children sequence the stories. Children might take the sheet home and tell the story and act it for their parents.

The Little Red Hen

WAYS TO DRAMATIZE
THE LITTLE RED HEN

1. Read the story and chant the bold words with the children while doing the action.

2. Use props as you act the story with the children: sheaves of wheat (available at floral supply stores) and a few grains of wheat from them (for the seed); kitchen utensils, such as a bowl and spoon; flour and a loaf of bread.

3. Dramatize the story as a play choosing children to play the hen, cat, mouse, and goose. Several children play the growing wheat. Add more roles by having a miller. Two might play the oven; two, the mill, and one or two the bowl. Others might be "prop bearers" handing the hen such props as a pan. NOTE: To make the bread appear, the oven actors turn their backs (as if closing the oven door) as the hen hands them an empty pan. When the bread is done, they place the bread in the pan so that the audience cannot see it, and it is revealed when they turn around and she opens the door.

4. Use a Sound Crew to play rhythm instruments. For example, strike a wood block crisply when the hen walks; ring jingle bells for the cat's meows; strike a wood block for the mouse's nibbles: and honk a bike horn for the goose's honks. Use rattles or maracas for the mill grinding and for shaking ingredients into the bowl. Ring bells or wind chimes when the bread appears and when she eats, "Yum, yum."

HINTS TO DEVELOP LANGUAGE

1. Color your speech to make the words resemble the sounds they describe. For example, say "Dig..." emphasizing the explosive *d* and *g* to make it sound like thrusting a shovel into hard earth. Open your eyes wide and stretch out the letters in "br–ea–d" making it sound soft, warm, and delicious.

2. Change your voice for each character. Use a perky voice for the hen, a light carefree voice for the cat, a high squeaky one for the mouse, and a nasal harsh one for the goose.

Cluck, cluck, cluck, cluck.

☞ *flap wings*

One day a little red hen looked with her big eyes and saw

a seed, a seed, a seed, a seed.

☞ *point at seed*

3

And she said,

"Wow! Wow! Wow! WOW!"

☞ *open wings in wonder*

She asked, "Who will help

plant, plant, plant, plant

this seed?"

☞ *point at ground*

4

"Not I,"
said the cat.

Meow, meow, meow, meow.

👉 *shake head and paws, "no"*

"Not I,"
said the mouse.

Nibble, nibble, nibble, nibble.

👉 *shake head "no" and nibble cheese*

"Not I,"
said the goose.

Honk, honk, honk, honk.

👉 *toss head "no"*

"Then I'll plant it

myself, myself, myself, myself."

☞ *stamp foot*

And she

digs, digs, digs, digs.

☞ *dig*

And she waters

shh, shh, shh, shh.

☞ *water seed*

6

And the seed
began to grow.

☞ *become seed, hide head*

One, two, three, four...

☞ *count to four, kneel and sprout*

five, six, seven, eight.

☞ *keep counting, rise and become tall wheat*

Sway, sway, sway, sway.

☞ *sway slowly in the breeze*

7

When the seed was grown, the Little Red Hen asked, "Who will help me cut this

wheat, wheat, wheat, wheat?"

☞ *point at the big wheat field*

"Not I," said the cat.

Meow, meow, meow, meow.

"Not I," said the mouse.

Nibble, nibble, nibble, nibble.

"Not I," said the goose.

Honk, honk, honk, honk.

"Then I'll cut it

MYSELF, MYSELF, MYSELF, MYSELF."

 *stamp foot*

9

cut, cut, cut, cut.

☞ *cut wheat*

When the wheat was cut, the Little Red Hen asked, "Who will help me take the wheat to the

mill, mill, mill, mill?"

☞ *make a big round mill with arms*

"Not I," said the cat.

Meow, meow, meow, meow.

"Not I," said the mouse.

Nibble, nibble, nibble, nibble.

"Not I," said the goose.

Honk, honk, honk, honk.

"Then I'll take it

MYSELF, MYSELF, MYSELF, MYSELF."

☞ *stamp foot*

11

And she

walks, walks, walks, walks

to the mill.

☞ *walk like a hen*

And the mill

grinds, grinds, grinds, grinds.

☞ *spin hands like the mill wheel*

And she got a bag of

flour, flour, flour, flour.

☞ *show flour proudly*

And she

walks, walks, walks, walks

home.

☞ *walk like a hen*

When she got home, the Little Red Hen asked, "Who will help me make this flour into

bread, bread, bread, bread?"

☞ *smack lips excitedly*

> "Not I," said the cat.

Meow, meow, meow, meow.

> "Not I," said the mouse.

Nibble, nibble, nibble, nibble.

> "Not I," said the goose.

Honk, honk, honk, honk.

> "Then I'll make it

MYSELF, MYSELF, MYSELF, MYSELF."

☞ *stamp foot*

And she got a

**bowl, bowl,
bowl, bowl.**

☞ *show bowl proudly*

And she put in flour.

**Shh, shh,
shh, shh.**

☞ *shake in flour*

She put in salt.

**Ch, ch,
ch, ch.**

☞ *shake salt*

She put in milk.

**Glug, glug,
glug, glug.**

☞ *pour milk*

And she

**stirs, stirs,
stirs, stirs.**

☞ *stir*

17

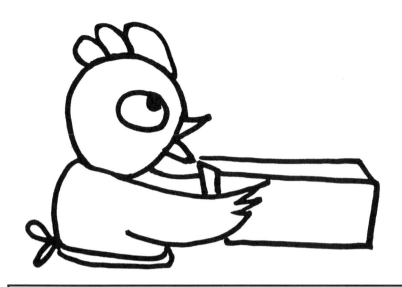

She got a

**pan, pan,
pan, pan.**

☞ *show pan proudly*

She put the dough into the pan.

**Kerplop,
kerplop,
kerplop,
kerplop.**

☞ *plop dough in*

And she

**kneads,
kneads,
kneads,
kneads.**

☞ *knead dough*

Then she

walks, walks, walks, walks

to the oven.

☞ *walk like a hen*

She put the pan into the oven.

☞ *set pan in*

And she

waits, waits, waits, waits.

☞ *pace like a hen*

And she

sniffs, sniffs, sniffs, sniffs.

☞ *say mmmmmmm*

And she looked into the oven and said,

"Wow! Wow! Wow! Wow!"

☞ *show excitement*

She took the pan out of the oven and had a

beautiful, beautiful, beautiful, beautiful

loaf of bread!

And she asked,
"Who will help me EAT this

**bread, bread,
bread, bread?"**

☞ *raise bread high*

21

"I WILL,"
said the cat.

Meow, meow, meow, meow.

☞ *nod head and paws "yes"*

"I WILL,"
said the mouse.

Nibble, nibble, nibble, nibble.

☞ *nod head "yes" and nibble cheese*

"I WILL,"
said the goose.

Honk, honk, honk, honk.

☞ *nod head and flap wings "yes"*

22

> But the Little Red Hen
> said, "NO!" She said,

"No, no,
no, NO!"

👉 *shake head and wing tip "NO"*

23

The Little Red Hen asked, "Who FOUND the

seed, seed, seed, seed?"

"Who PLANTED the seed?"

Dig, dig, dig, dig.

"Who WATERED the seed?"

Shh, shh, shh, shh.

"Who CUT the wheat?"

**Cut, cut,
cut, cut.**

"Who WALKED to the mill?"

**Walk, walk,
walk, walk.**

"I DID! I DID! I DID! I DID!"

☞ *point at self proudly*

> "Then, who will
> EAT the bread?

**Not you, not you,
not, you, not you."**

**Boo hoo
hoo hoo.**

**Boo hoo
hoo hoo.**

**Boo hoo
hoo hoo.**

Yum, yum, yum, yum.

☞ *eat with pleasure mmmmm!*

TEACHER'S GUIDE *The Little Red Hen*

LANGUAGE ARTS

These **Critical Thinking Questions** are divided into categories according to educational researcher B. S. Bloom's "Taxonomy," a questioning system to develop higher order thinking in students. Categories begin with the most concrete, remembering the facts in the story, and go to the most abstract, evaluating the story to determine its worth.

Educators Lawrence Kohlberg and Hilda Taba and Psychologist Robert Coles believe in the value of developing moral and social awareness. This traditional British folk tale addresses the ethical themes of the value of hard work and persistence, the importance of cooperation, self esteem, and enjoying the fruits of one's labors. Questions on these themes are grouped under **Moral Reasoning Questions**.

Knowledge
1. Where does the story take place?
2. What are five interesting action words in the story?
3. Who are the characters in the story?

Comprehension
1. Why doesn't the hen yell at the animals when they won't help her?
2. Why does the hen eat the bread in front of the animals?
3. Do you think the animals will ever help the hen? Explain.

Application
1. Who helps you every day? What does that person do to help you? What might you do to help that person?
2. If you were the boss of a store, how would you get the cat, mouse, and goose to do their work?
3. Is there any work you like doing? What is it?

Analysis
1. Give a different ending to the story. Why would you end it like that?
2. Tell three ways in which the hen is like you.
3. Does the story have a happy or sad ending? Explain.

Synthesis
1. When the hen saw the seed, she got an idea that it could become bread. Artists have ideas too. What idea do you have of something you'd like to paint about the story?

Evaluation
1. This is an old story, and many people have liked it. What makes this a good story?
2. Who is your favorite character in the story? What do you like about that character?
3. Do you think the story ends the way it should? Explain.

Moral Reasoning Questions
1. Why does the hen continue to work when no one will help her?
2. Do you think the hen was unkind not to give the cat, mouse, and goose bread? Explain.
3. Some say the hen feels proud at the end of the story. What makes her feel proud?
4. Would you have given the bread to the animals? Explain.

SCIENCE

Understanding wheat by studying and then becoming a growing wheat plant
First, sprout some wheat grass (available in pet and health food stores). Then, do the following "Growing into a Wheat Plant" activity.

- First become a grain buried deep in the cold winter ground. You are small and hard. Then, you feel the rain come through the soil and onto you. Now the sun casts its warm rays through the soil, and you begin to sprout. On a slow count to five, you push slowly through your seed jacket.
- Keep counting to ten as you feel your roots push down, and you grow into a wheat plant. Finally, you are a tall wheat plant with beautiful golden grain on you. Make your fingers into tall stalks of grain.
- Sway slowly in the breeze. You are just like the beautiful "amber waves of grain" in the song, "America the Beautiful." What color is amber? Why is the wheat called "amber waves of grain?"

SOCIAL SCIENCE AND HEALTH

Discovering the importance of wheat
The Little Red Hen makes flour from wheat. Wheat is one of the most important food plants in this country. Wheat grows in the midwest. Locate on a map the great wheat-growing areas. Then, answer the following questions about wheat and its uses.

1. Why do people eat bread?
2. What nutritional value does wheat bread have?
3. How is wheat made into flour to make bread?
4. How many types of breads can you name?
5. What is your favorite type of bread?
6. What kind of food do you like to eat with bread?

MATH

Making Bread: A Measurement Activity
Find a simple bread recipe. Write the ingredients on the board with the measurements. Students measure, mix and bake the bread as directed by the teacher.

FINE ARTS

Making a Hen's Comb
Students cut a hen's comb from red paper. The teacher pastes or staples the comb to the center of a sentence strip and then staple the headband to fit the child. The child dramatizes the story wearing their red hen comb.

APPRECIATING AND EXPERIENCING CLASSICAL MUSIC

Have students listen to "The Cocks and Chicks" section of *The Carnival of Animals* by Camille Saint-Saens and then respond to the following:

1. How does the music make you feel?
2. In what way does the music sound like the hen in the story?
3. Why do you think this type of music is good for this story?
4. What instruments do you hear? Choose an instrument that you like and pretend to play it with the orchestra.
5. Move your arms, hands and fingers to conduct the music.

Adult: Have children discuss and re-enact the actions in the pictures. They might also discuss and act the hen's other chores. For sequencing, have them cut the pictures apart and paste them in order or number them using the squares in each box.

The end.

The Lion and the Mouse

WAYS TO DRAMATIZE
THE LION AND THE MOUSE

1. Read the story and chant the bold words with the children while doing the action.

2. Let all of the children play the mouse with each wearing simple mouse ears while you, an aide, or an older student take the role of the lion wearing yellow nylon netting as a mane.

3. Develop the story into a play. Increase the number of roles by having three children play palm trees; two play hunters; and four, berry bushes. Add simple costumes such as blue nylon fabric wiggled for a lake, a green feather boa for a tree, and red gloves for berry bushes. Have one of more older children tell the story or read from the book.

HINTS TO DEVELOP LANGUAGE

1. Use rhythm instruments to accent the language's musicality. For example, strike a drum firmly for the lion's "paw, paw, paw, paw"; strike a wood block lightly for the mouse's "scurry..."; jingle bells for the lake's "shimmer..."; strike a triangle for the palm tree's sway and for plucking berries from a bush— "one, two, three, four." Shake rattles lightly as the hunter, "sneaks..." and briskly as the lion says, "roar..." thrashing in the net.

2. Color your speech to make the words resemble what they describe. Add a gesture to emphasize the meaning. Say, "Shimmer, shimmer..." highlighting the delicate quality of the moving lake; say, "paw, paw..." stressing the *p* and the lion's powerful movement. Elongate the *ay* in "Sway" as you bend in the breeze.

3. Change your voice for each character. Use a strong, low voice for the mighty lion; a high, squeaky one for the vulnerable mouse; a treacherous menacing one for the hunter.

One day a big lion came pawing along.

**Paw, paw,
paw, paw.**

☞ *walk like a lion*

He saw a shimmering lake.

Shimmer, shimmer, shimmer, shimmer.

☞ *shimmer*

The lion pawed to the lake.

Paw, paw, paw, paw.

☞ *walk like a lion*

He licked the water with his long lion tongue.

Lick, lick, lick, lick.

☞ *lick the cool water*

He saw a swaying palm tree.

Sway, sway, sway, sway.

☞ *sway like the palm*

The lion stretched out his body and fell asleep.

Zzzz, zzzz, zzzz, zzzz.

☞ *stretch and sleep*

39

In the meantime, a mouse
popped out of her mouse house.

Pop, pop,
pop, pop.

☞ *pop up four times*

She scurried into the jungle.

Scurry, scurry,
scurry, scurry.

☞ *scurry*

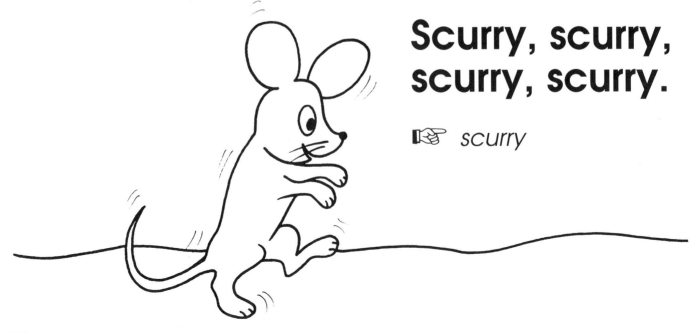

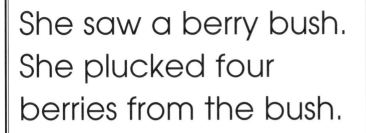

She saw a berry bush.
She plucked four
berries from the bush.

☞ become a bush,
pluck four berries

**One, two,
three, four.**

She nibbled each one.

**Nibble, nibble,
nibble, nibble.**

☞ nibble each berry

41

She saw a
shimmering lake.

**Shimmer, shimmer,
shimmer, shimmer.**

☞ *shimmer*

She scurried
to the lake.

**Scurry, scurry,
scurry, scurry.**

☞ *scurry*

She licked the water
with her tiny tongue.

**Lick, lick,
lick, lick.**

☞ *lick the water*

42

She scurried toward the palm tree.

Scurry, scurry, scurry, scurry.

☞ *scurry*

But accidentally, she put her

paw, paw, paw, paw

☞ *touch the lion*

on the lion.

He awoke with a

ROAR, ROAR, ROAR, ROAR!

☞ *roar*

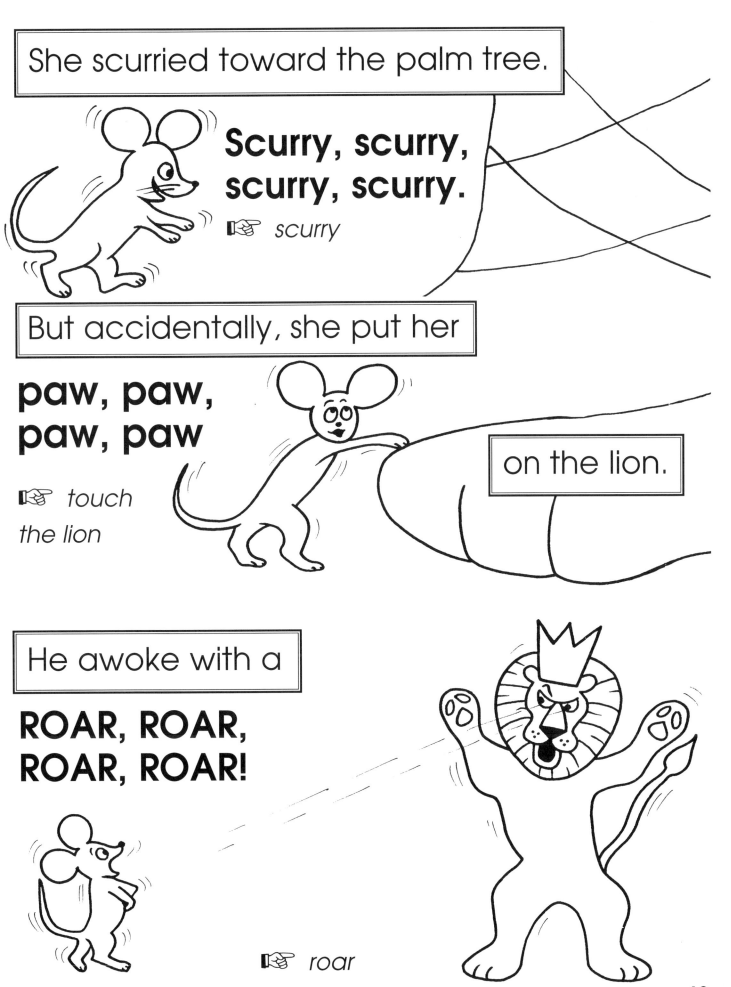

He pointed at the mouse and said,

**"I'm going to eat you,
I'm going to eat you,
I'm going to eat you,
I'm going to eat you."**

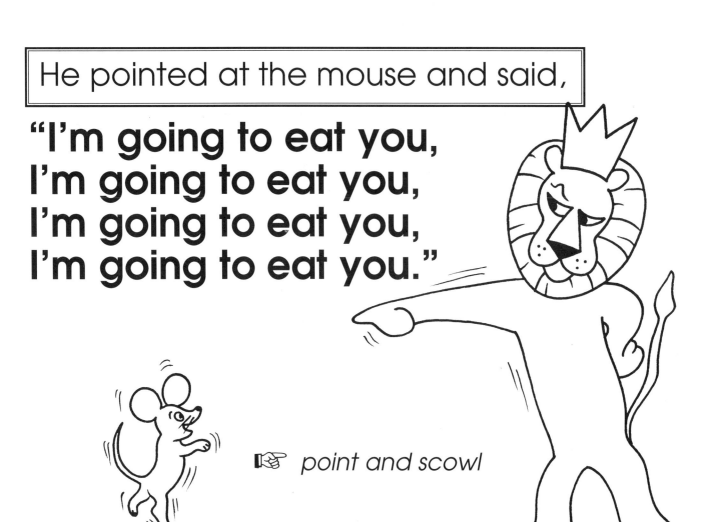

☞ *point and scowl*

The mouse trembled and trembled and said,

**"No! No!
No! NO!"**

☞ *tremble
and shake
head "No!"*

The lion roared,

"Why not? Why not? Why not? Why not?"

☞ *stamp foot*

The mouse said, "Maybe someday I can

**help you,
help you,
help you,
help you."**

☞ *bob head hopefully*

> The lion raised one paw and laughed.

**HA! HA!
HA! HA!**

☞ *raise paw and laugh*

> He raised two paws
> and laughed louder.

**HA! HA!
HA! HA!**

☞ *raise two paws
and laugh louder*

> Finally, his whole
> body shook and
> laughed.

**HA! HA!
HA! HA!**

☞ *shake and laugh
loudest of all*

He pointed and said, "How can a little animal like you help a BIG ANIMAL like

me, me, me, ME?"

 *point at your big self 4 times*

The mouse said,

"Maybe, maybe, maybe, maybe

I could."

 *bob head hopefully*

The lion said, "That's so funny I'm going to let you

go! Go! Go! Go!"

☞ *shoo the mouse with a paw*

The mouse said,

"Thank you, thank you, thank you, thank you."

☞ *bow gratefully*

She scurried toward her home.

Scurry, scurry, scurry, scurry.

☞ *scurry*

But first, she raised a paw and said, "I won't forget my

promise, promise, promise, promise."

☞ *raise a paw*

The lion shook his mane, stretched out his body and fell into a d-e-e-p sleep.

ZZZZZ, ZZZZZ, ZZZZZ, ZZZZZ. ☞ *shake your mane, sleep, and dream*

In the meantime, a bad hunter came sneaking into the jungle.

Sneak, sneak, sneak, sneak.

☞ *sneak "in place"*

He had a big

net, net, net, net.

☞ *display net proudly*

He pointed at the lion and whispered,

"See that lion.
See that lion.
See that lion.
See that lion."

☞ *point and whisper*

"I'm going to get him with my

net, net, net, net."

☞ *display net proudly*

Then he went

sneak,
sneak,
sneak,
sneak

to
the
lion.

☞ *sneak*

51

He tossed the net over the lion

one, two, three, four.

☞ *toss net over lion*

Then he went to get a wagon to take the lion to the circus.

Sneak, sneak, sneak, sneak.

☞ *sneak away*

Then the lion awoke.
He clawed one part of
the net and roared.

**ROAR, ROAR,
ROAR, ROAR.**

☞ *claw and roar*

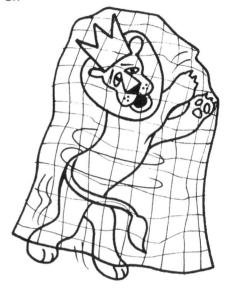

He clawed another
part and roared.

**ROAR, ROAR,
ROAR, ROAR.**

☞ *claw and roar louder*

He clawed all over
and roared.

**ROAR! ROAR!
ROAR! ROAR!**

☞ *claw and roar loudest*

The mouse heard the roar and said, "I know that

**roar, roar,
roar, roar."**

☞ *cock head and listen*

She scurried to the lion.

**Scurry, scurry,
scurry, scurry.**

☞ *scurry*

She nibbled one
part of the net.

**Nibble, nibble,
nibble, nibble.**

☞ *nibble*

She nibbled another
part of the net.

**Nibble, nibble,
nibble, nibble.**

☞ *nibble harder*

She nibbled all over the net.

**Nibble, nibble,
nibble, nibble.**

☞ *nibble*
hardest
of all

The lion could hear the hunter returning and said,

"Hurry up! Hurry up! Hurry up! Hurry up!"

☞ *speak urgently*

Just when the hunter returned, the lion sprang at the hunter.

ROAR, ROAR, ROAR, ROAR.

☞ *spring and roar*

The hunter froze in terror. He opened his mouth and yelled,

"Help! Help! Help! Help!"

☞ *throw up hands, open mouth wide, and freeze*

Then, the little mouse bowed to the king and said, "I was happy to serve your

majesty, majesty, majesty, majesty."

☞ *bow*

But the big lion said, "NO, I'm going to bow to

you, you, you, you!"

☞ *bow humbly*

He said, "You've shown me that the littlest thing can be the most wonderful in all of the

world, world, world, world."

☞ *open up paws in wonder*

Then the big lion presented the little mouse with a golden

crown, crown, crown, crown.

☞ *put crown carefully on your little head*

60

They posed to show that they would be friends.

Forever more, forever more, forever more, forever more.

☞ pose and put a paw on a new or old friend

They were so happy.
First Lion sang his Lion Song.

☞ *sing to tune of "Frère Jacques"*

I am lion. I am lion.
Roar, roar, roar.
Roar, roar, roar.
I am lion. I am lion.
Roar, roar, roar.
Roar, roar, roar.

Mouse sang her Mouse song.

☞ *sing to same tune*

I am mouse. I am mouse.
Squeak, squeak, squeak.
Squeak, squeak, squeak.
I am mouse. I am mouse.
Squeak, squeak, squeak.
Squeak, squeak, squeak.

Finally, the two friends walked

side by side, side by side, side by side, side by side

through the jungle singing their friendship song.

☞ *sing to same tune*

We are friends. We are friends.
Squeak, squeak, roar.
Squeak, squeak, roar.
We are friends. We are friends.
Forever more. Forever more.

TEACHER'S GUIDE *The Lion and the Mouse*

LANGUAGE ARTS

These **Critical Thinking Questions** are divided into categories according to educational researcher B. S. Bloom's "Taxonomy," a questioning system to develop higher order thinking in students. Categories begin with the most concrete, remembering the facts in the story, and go to the most abstract, evaluating the story to determine its worth.

Educators Lawrence Kohlberg and Hilda Taba and Psychologist Robert Coles believe in the value of developing moral and social awareness. This Greek fable addresses several ethical themes that lend themselves to the development of moral and social awareness.

These themes include: beware of hubris or overweening pride, a feeling that you can lord it over those smaller or more vulnerable than yourself; honor promises made no matter how difficult; and appreciate those of different types for they can add qualities to your life that you lack and enrich you. Questions on these themes are grouped under **Moral Reasoning Questions.**

Knowledge
1. Tell me three actions of the lion in the story.
2. Tell me three actions of the mouse in the story.
3. What did the mouse do that made the lion angry?
4. Tell me something exciting that happens in the story.
5. Tell me something funny that happens in the story.

Comprehension
1. Why weren't the lion and the mouse friends at the beginning of the story?
2. Why does the lion laugh at the mouse when she says someday she might help him?
3. Why does the mouse help the lion?

Application
1. Tell me three things a mouse can do that you can do.
2. Tell me three things a lion can do that you can do.
3. Tell me three things you can do that a mouse or lion can not do.

Analysis
1. Tell three ways in which the mouse in the story is like you.
2. Tell me how the mouse and lion are different. How are they the same?
3. What parts of this story could happen in real life? What parts could not happen?

Synthesis
1. Tell me three things you can do to make a friend.
2. Tell me three things you can do to be a good friend to your pet.
3. If you were making costumes for a play, what kind of people clothes would you put on the lion and mouse? Draw a picture of the lion and mouse in people clothes.

Evaluation
1. Who is your favorite character in the story? Why do you like this character best?
2. What is your favorite part of the story? Why do you like this part best?
3. This fable is one of the oldest stories in the world. Why do people continue to like it after all these years?
4. If you could be a character in this story, which character would you be and why?

Moral Reasoning Questions

1. Why do some people say it's unkind to make fun of another person the way the lion does to the mouse?
2. Some people say the mouse is tiny, but she is also strong. In what way is the mouse in the story strong?
3. *The Lion and the Mouse* is a fable. Fables often teach a lesson to a character in the story. What does the lion learn in the story?
4. The lion is called "King of the Jungle." Kings used to rule countries. Do you think it's good to have a king telling people what to do? Explain.
5. Some people say it's not right to put lions in zoos or circuses. What do you think? Explain.
6. At the end of the story, the lion bows humbly to the mouse. What does "humbly" mean? Why does the lion bow "humbly?"
7. The mouse keeps her promise. What is a promise? Why is it important to keep promises?

SCIENCE

Understanding Lions and Mice by Studying and Then Becoming Them

Share the Lion and Mouse Information with the students and show them pictures of the real animals. Then have them do the Becoming the Animal activities to experience the animals' physical attributes and activities.

Studying and Understanding Lions

Lion Information: Lions have big golden manes and fur, and long tails and bodies. They have strong claws and long sharp teeth for grabbing prey and ripping into it. They sleep up to 20 hours a day when their stomachs are full. Lions have a roar that can be heard for four miles. Even though they live on grassy plains, they are called King of the Jungle.

Becoming Lions

- Stretch out your beautiful long golden legs and paw slowly over the golden grassy plains.
- Raise your front legs and paws high into the air, extend your claws, and sharpen them on a tree trunk.
- Paw along looking for food. See some prey. Pounce on it with your strong shoulders. Rip into the meat with your long sharp teeth.
- You're thirsty. Paw to the lake. Put your big head down and lap, lap, lap the cool water with your long, rough, lion tongue.
- Now, you're tired. Shake your big golden mane. Stretch out your long lion legs. Put your big beautiful head down and fall fast asleep.

Studying and Understanding Mice

Mouse Information: Mice are small and quick with big alert eyes, noses that are always quivering, and big ears to warn them of enemies. They have long blunt front teeth for gnawing berries and nuts, and tiny paws that can pluck and hold things.

Becoming Mice

- Show yourself hiding in your mouse hole under the ground.
- Poke your head out and look to left and right and up above for enemies.
- Sniff all around.
- Scurry out lightly in place. See a raspberry bush. Pluck one, two, three, four sweet berries and nibble them. Keep sniffing and looking around.
- Lick water from a puddle.
- Wash berry juice off your paws with your little mouse tongue.
- Look up and see a big owl hovering above. Squeak and quiver in fear. Scurry quickly back to your mouse hole, pull yourself in tight and pant in fear. Feel your tiny heart go "pat, pat, pat."
- Peek out to see if the owl has gone. Yes, he has. Curl up tight and go to sleep.

FINE ARTS AND MULTICULTURAL AWARENESS

Creating a paper-plate African Mask of the Lion
Materials: Paper plate, fast-drying glue, paint, crayon, or magic markers, materials for decoration such as different kinds of pasta, dried beans, shells, beads, yarn, ribbon, fabric, and colored paper; tape and string if the mask is to be worn.

Method: Show students a book of African masks. Point out that these masks don't exactly look like the animal, but capture its feeling. Ask students to note the different patterns on the masks and how the patterns make the eyes stand out. Ask, "Why do you think the artist makes the eyes stand out?"

Have students bring in materials from home. Students might make a sketch of their mask, planning where to put the different decorations. Have students determine where the eye holes should be on their masks and cut them out. They should paint the eyes first to make them stand out. Students may add ears by using part of another plate.

If students want to wear their mask, show them how to attach an elastic band or string. If students act or dance with their masks, the movements of their bodies must be exaggerated to show the character's actions and feelings. Students may want to look at pictures or see a video of people dancing with animal masks. They then might make up a simple lion circle dance—pawing in one direction and then the other and going inside and out raising and lowering their paws.

APPRECIATING AND EXPERIENCING CLASSICAL MUSIC

Have students listen to "The Lion" section of *The Carnival of Animals* by Camille Saint-Saens and respond to the following:
1. How does the music make you feel?
2. In what way does the music sound like the lion in the story?
3. Why do you think this type of music is good for this story?
4. What instruments do you hear? Choose an instrument that you like and pretend to play it with the orchestra.
5. Move your arms, hands, and fingers to conduct the music.

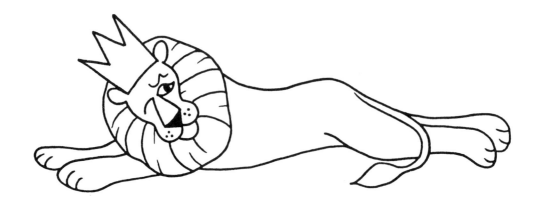

Adult: Have children discuss and re-enact the actions in the pictures. They might also discuss and act the character's other actions. For sequencing, have them cut the pictures apart and paste them in order or number them using the squares in each box.

67

The end. The end.

The Three Billy Goats Gruff

WAYS TO DRAMATIZE
THE THREE BILLY GOATS GRUFF

1. Read the story and chant the bold words with the children while doing the action.

2. Develop the story into a play. For younger children, each child decides which of the three goats or the troll to play. Assign each goat group its own space and make a bridge of carpet squares in the center of the room. Each goat crosses the bridge on its turn, and the troll group sits by the bridge and plays its part.

3. Or cast individuals to play each individual goat and the troll. Increase the roles by having several play the bridge clasping hands in a line like a railing and having the goats trot in front of them. Two play frogs who croak when the troll chants. Two are the water under the bridge using light blue fabric that is tossed over the troll when he disappears. Others are happy trees, flowers and the sun.

4. Add simple costumes. Attach horns of different sizes to a tagboard head band for each goat. Or use hats—a beanie for the little goat with pink Post-its for budding horns, a baseball cap with middle-sized horns for the middle sized goat and a derby or other adult hat with big curved horns for the big goat. Attach green yarn to a rolled up paper bag for the troll.

HINTS TO DEVELOP LANGUAGE

1. Color your speech to make the words resemble what they describe. Say, "Shiver, shiver..." highlighting the nervous fear of the goats; say "Trip, trap..." stressing the clipped *t* and *p* of the prancing hooves.

2. Use rhythm or homemade instruments to accent the language and the action. Tap a woodblock lightly, moderately, or strongly to simulate the "trip-trap" sound of each goat. Shake rattles as the goats' say, "chew, chew, chew," and for their "grass song." Jingle bells to highlight their "joy..." as they leap happily. Use a rainstick or wind chimes as they sleep.

Once there were three billy goats.
Their name was Gruff.

One, two, three goats,
One, two, three goats,
One, two, three goats,
One, two, three goats.

☞ *Chant "one, two, three" showing a finger for each goat.*
Make horns on your head on the word "goats."

The first was a

little, little,
little, little

goat.

☞ *make voice and body little, make little horns*

The second was a

middle,
middle,
middle,
middle-sized

goat.

☞ *make voice and body middle-sized, make middle-sized horns*

The third was a

big, big,
big, big

goat.

☞ *make voice and body big, make big horns*

The goats loved to chew grass. And as they chewed, they sang their grass song.

Chew, chew, chew green grass.
Chew it all day long.
Chew, chew chew green grass.
It makes us big and strong.

☞ *sing to the tune of "Row, Row, Row Your Boat,"*
chew grass and open and close fingers to look like chewing,
show big muscles on "big and strong"

The goats were

happy, happy,
happy, happy.

☞ *place hoofs at sides*
of face and smile

But one day, they looked and saw no more grass. They felt

sad, sad, sad, sad.

☞ *shake head sadly*

They felt so **hungry, hungry, hungry, hungry.**

☞ *look sad and pat empty stomach four times*

**bridge,
bridge,
bridge,
bridge.**

☞ *make a big bridge with arms*

**grass, grass,
grass, grass.**

☞ *wiggle fingers like grass blowing in the breeze*

But under the bridge lived an ugly

troll, troll, troll, troll.

☞ *make an ugly face, grow ugly hands, and growl*

He had cruel

eyes, eyes, eyes, eyes.

☞ *show cruel eyes*

He had a big sniffing

nose, nose, nose, nose.

☞ *sniff all around*

He had sharp

teeth, teeth, teeth, teeth.

☞ *show sharp teeth*

78

The goats knew the Troll lived there. And they

shivered,
shivered,
shivered,
shivered.

☞ *shiver*

But the three goats were

wise, wise,
wise, wise.

☞ *point to head wisely four times*

79

They said to each other,

"Come here! Come here! Come here! Come here!"

☞ *beckon with an arm*

They began to

talk, talk, talk, talk.

☞ *lean forward and pretend to talk*

They got a good

idea, idea, idea, idea.

☞ *point above head*

80

First, the little goat started over the bridge.

Trip-trap, trip-trap, trip-trap, trip-trap

went his little hooves on the bridge.

Trip

Trap

Trap Trip

☞ *make little finger taps on legs and speak in a little voice*

"WHO is that tripping and trapping over MY

bridge, bridge, bridge, bridge?"

roared the Troll.

☞ *shake finger and roar*

81

"It is I, the

little, little, little, little

goat. I'm going across the bridge to eat green grass."

☞ *make voice and body little*

But the Troll roared, "Oh, NO, you are NOT. I'm coming up to

EAT YOU!
EAT YOU!
EAT YOU!
EAT YOU!"

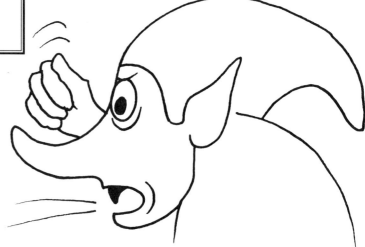

☞ *shake a fist and roar*

"No! No! No! No!"

said the little goat.

"Please don't do that. Wait for the middle-sized goat. He's much bigger and fatter than I am."

☞ *speak humbly in a little voice*

"All right, but

HURRY,
HURRY,
HURRY,
HURRY,"

roared the Troll.

☞ *roar and shoo the goat away*

And the little goat went

trip-trap, trip-trap,
trip-trap, trip-trap

over the bridge.

☞ *make little finger taps and speak in a little voice*

83

Then, the middle-sized goat started across the bridge.

Trip-trap, trip-trap, trip-trap, trip-trap

went his middle-sized hooves on the bridge.

☞ *make middle-sized taps and speak in a middle-sized voice*

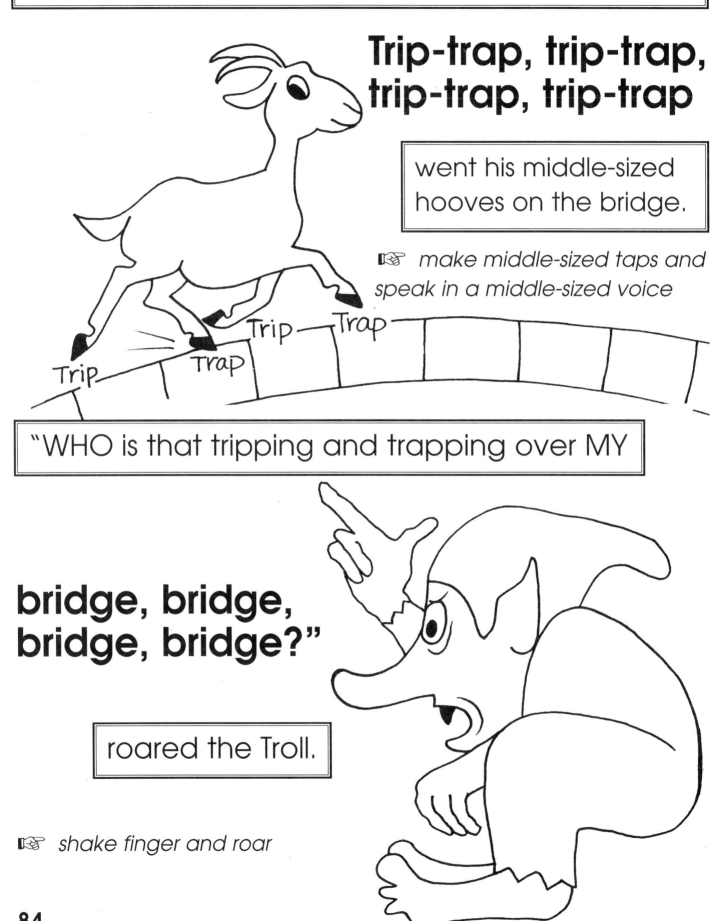

Trip Trap Trip Trap

"WHO is that tripping and trapping over MY

bridge, bridge, bridge, bridge?"

roared the Troll.

☞ *shake finger and roar*

84

"It is I, the

**middle,
middle,
middle,
middle-sized**

goat. I'm going across the bridge to eat green grass."

☞ *make voice and body little*

But the Troll roared, "Oh, NO, you are NOT. I'm coming up to

EAT YOU! EAT YOU! EAT YOU! EAT YOU!"

The middle-sized goat said,

"No! No! No! No!"

☞ *shake a fist and roar*

"Please don't do that. Wait for the big goat. He's much bigger and fatter than I am."

"All right, but

**HURRY,
HURRY,
HURRY,
HURRY,"**

roared the Troll.

☞ *roar and shoo
the goat away*

And the middle-sized goat went

**trip-trap, trip-trap,
trip-trap, trip-trap**

over the bridge.

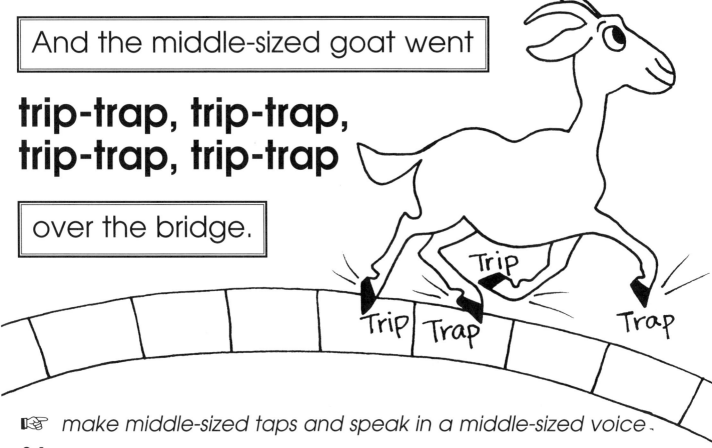

Trip

Trip Trap Trap

☞ *make middle-sized taps and speak in a middle-sized voice.*

Finally, the big goat started across the bridge.

Trip-trap, trip-trap, trip-trap, trip-trap

went his big hooves on the bridge.

☞ make big claps and speak in a big voice

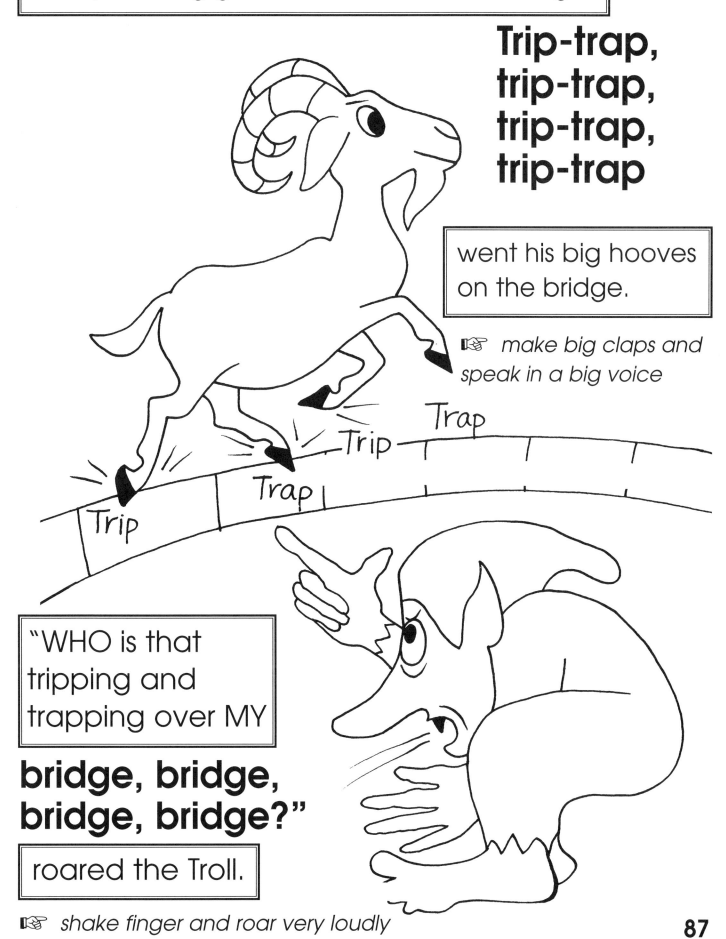

"WHO is that tripping and trapping over MY

bridge, bridge, bridge, bridge?"

roared the Troll.

☞ shake finger and roar very loudly

"Come right along," said the big goat, "and I'll knock you with my

horns, horns, horns, horns."

☞ *show big horns*

The Troll poked his ugly head

up, up, up, up

over the bridge.

☞ *poke head up*

But the big goat lowered his horns and butted the Troll

**up, up,
up, up**

into the air.

P o w!!!

☞ *knock the bad*
Troll with horns

90

spinning, spinning, spinning, spinning.

☞ *spin in circles or twirl arms*

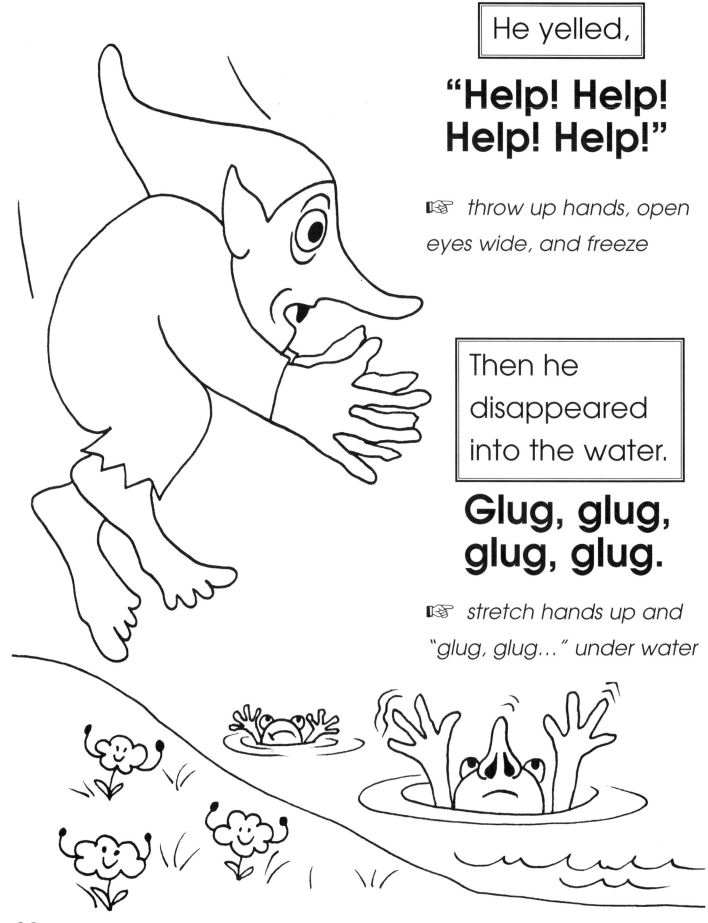

He yelled,

"Help! Help! Help! Help!"

☞ *throw up hands, open eyes wide, and freeze*

Then he disappeared into the water.

Glug, glug, glug, glug.

☞ *stretch hands up and "glug, glug..." under water*

Then, the big goat went

**trip-trap, trip-trap,
trip-trap, trip-trap**

over the bridge to join his brothers.

☞ *make big claps and
speak in a big voice*

The three brothers bleated and leaped with

joy, joy, joy, joy.

☞ *leap joyfully and bleat, "Maa"*

Then they trotted up the hill. They ate delicious green grass and sang their grass song.

Chew, chew, chew green grass.
Chew it all day long.
Chew, chew chew green grass.
It makes us big and strong.

☞ *sing to the tune of "Row, Row, Row Your Boat"*
open and close fingers to look like chewing,
and show big muscles on "big and strong"

Finally, they felt so

full, full, full, full.

☞ *pat full stomach*

They sang their sleeping song.

We will sleep now. We will sleep now.
We walked so far. We walked so far.
We will sleep now. We will sleep now.
Under a star. Under a star.

☞ *sing to tune of "Frère Jacques"*

Finally, they lay down on the green grass. They closed their eyes and dreamed happy dreams.

ZZZZ, ZZZZ,
ZZZZ, ZZZZ.

☞ *sleep and dream of green grass and happy days*

TEACHER'S GUIDE *The Three Billy Goats Gruff*

LANGUAGE ARTS

These questions are divided into categories according to educational researcher B. S. Bloom's Taxonomy, a system to develop higher order thinking. Categories begin with the concrete, remembering the facts in the story, and go to the abstract, evaluating the story to determine its worth.

Educators Lawrence Kohlberg and Hilda Taba and Harvard Psychologist Robert Coles believe in the value of developing moral and social awareness. This traditional Norwegian tale addresses the themes of loyalty, friendship, and cooperation. Questions on these issues are grouped under **Moral Reasoning Questions**.

Knowledge
1. What do the goats like to eat?
2. Why must the goats cross the bridge?
3. What makes the goats shiver with fear?
4. What sound do the hooves of the goats make when they cross the bridge?
5. What happens to the Troll at the end of the story?

Comprehension
1. Why are the goats happy in the beginning of the story?
2. Why must the goats trick the Troll?
3. Why do the goats come together and talk before crossing the bridge?
4. Why does the little goat cross the bridge first?
5. Why does the Troll live under a bridge?
6. Why do the goats leap with joy at the end of the story?

Application
1. Tell me three things that a goat can do and that you can do too.
2. Tell me something a goat does every day, but you wouldn't do it.
3. Could this story happen in the city or town where you live? Explain.

Analysis
1. Who is more clever: the Troll or the goats? Explain.
2. How do the goats trick the Troll?
3. Does this story have a sad or happy ending? Explain.

Synthesis
1. Tell me another good title for the story.
2. What might the goats say to each other before they cross the bridge?
3. Draw a picture of your favorite part of the story. Tell what is happening.

Evaluation
1. This story is old, and adults and children have liked it for many years. Why do you think people have liked this story for so many years?
2. Who is your favorite character in the story? Why do you like that character best?
3. Tell me something funny that happens in the story.
4. What part of the story is the most exciting?

Moral Reasoning Questions

1. The goats in the story are friends. What do the goats do that shows they are friends?
2. Why is it important to have friends?
3. Describe what a good friend does.
4. The goats speak politely to the Troll. What does it mean to speak politely?
5. The goats cooperate in the story. What is cooperation? How do the goats cooperate? Why is it important that they cooperated?

GEOGRAPHY AND SOCIAL SCIENCE

Share the following Norway information with students and bring in pictures to illustrate it. Then, have students locate Norway on the map, answer the questions, and do the social science-art activity.

Understanding Norway
Norway Information: Norway has many mountains, waterfalls, streams, green meadows, and fjords. It is far north and has lots of snow during its long winter.

In what way is the countryside of Norway different than the place where you live? Draw a picture of the goats on a Norway mountainside.

SCIENCE

Understanding Goats by Studying and Becoming Them
Share the Goat information with students and show them pictures of real goats. Then, have them do the Becoming Goats activities.

Goat Information: Goats have cloven hoofs and horns that curl back. They eat almost anything. They are light and agile and can leap from rock to rock on a mountainside. They produce milk which is used to drink and in cheese making.

One or two goats can supply milk for a family throughout the year. Goats are hardy and flourish better than cows in Norway's cold winters. Angora and cashmere groats are raised for their soft wool.

Male goats are called billys and usually have a beard. Females are called nannies. Baby goats are called kids.

Becoming a goat:
- Bite and chew grass for a long time.
- Drink water from a cool stream.
- In place, leap lightly three times and freeze with a cloven hoof in the air.
- You are a cashmere goat with extra soft fine fur. Stroke your beautiful fur.
- Now do three trip traps with your finger tips to show how light-footed you are.
- You are tired. Put your goat head on your desk and dream of beautiful green pastures.

FINE ARTS

Creating Goat Horns
Students cut a pair of backward curving horns to resemble those of real goats. (Study pictures.) Paste or staple the horns to the side of a sentence strip headband.

APPRECIATING AND EXPERIENCING CLASSICAL MUSIC

Have students listen to the "In the Hall of the Mountain King" section of *Grieg's Peer Gynt Suite* and then respond to the following:

1. How does the music make you feel?
2. In what way does the music sound like the characters in the story?
3. Why do you think this type of music is good for this story?
4. What instruments do you hear? Choose an instrument that you like and pretend to play it with the orchestra.
5. Move your arms, hands, and fingers to conduct the music.

101

THE THREE GRUFFS

SELECTED BIBLIOGRAPHY

LITERATURE DRAMATIZATION

Gerke, Pamela and Landalf, Helen. *Movement Stories for Children Ages 3–6*. Lyme, NH: Smith and Kraus, 1996. Detailed discussion on the importance of movement in children's development and a helpful explanation of movement concepts with ten active stories to be narrated for children to act.

Thistle, Louise. *Dramatizing Aesop's Fables*. Lyme, NH: Smith and Kraus, 1993. Aesop's Fables dramatized for the classroom or use on the stage. Includes acting techniques, character warm-ups, and critical thinking questions.

Thistle, Louise. *Dramatizing Classic Poetry for Middle and High School Students*, Lyme, NH: Smith and Kraus, 1999. More than fifty classic poems dramatized, with gestures, costume pieces and rhythm instruments to involve students completely in the poetry. Poems by Shakespeare, Langston Hughes, Emily Dickinson, Robert Frost, Edgar Allan Poe, William Blake, e.e. cummings, Christina Rosetti, and others.

Thistle, Louise. *Dramatizing Mother Goose: The Teacher's Guide to Play Acting in the Classroom, Preschool–Grade 2*. Lyme, NH: Smith and Kraus, 1998. Seventeen Mother Goose rhymes scripted to dramatize in the classroom and on stage. Costume and rhythm instrument suggestions, literature questions and historical background, and techniques to develop English Introduction to the study of nonsense verse and to performance for younger students.

Thistle, Louise. *Dramatizing Myths and Tales*. Lyme, NH: Smith and Kraus, 1995. Myths and tales dramatized from five cultures—West African, Mayan, Native American, Japanese, and British Isles. Includes detailed description of how to cast and direct beginning actors in a play.

COSTUMES

Hershberger, Priscilla. *Make Costumes for Creative Play*. Danbury, CT: Grolier Educational Corporation, 1993. Imaginative simple costumes with clear instructions on how to make them. Includes, for example, a tiger headdress made with an orange hand towel marked with felt tip pen and headbands using fabric trim. Wonderful color illustrations show how to make them.

MUSICAL INSTRUMENTS

West Music Company, 1212 5th Street, Coralville, IA 52241 (800-397-9378) A very complete catalogue of reasonably priced instruments. Also has books on teaching music and movement, silk scarves, and other materials helpful in dramatizing the stories in this book.

Fiarotta, Noel and Phyllis Fiarotta. *Music Crafts for Kids—The How-To Book of Music Discovery*. New York: Sterling Publishing Company, Inc., 1993. A charming book with a variety of information on music and the creation of simple instruments. Both students and teachers will enjoy this book.